Flirting With The Past

REYES CÁRDENAS

FLOWERSONG
PRESS

FlowerSong Press
McAllen, Texas 78501
Copyright © 2021 by Reyes Cárdenas

ISBN 978-1-953447-71-5
Library of Congress Control Number: 2021931089

Published by FlowerSong Press
in the United States of America.
www.flowersongpress.com

Set in Adobe Garamond Pro

Cover design by Matthew Revert
www.matthewrevert.com
Typeset by Elly Cridland
www.aeledapublishingservices.com

For the Future,
For My Grandchildren.

TABLE OF CONTENTS

Loving My Abuelo	1
Boris Karloff	3
Abuelo's Visit	4
My Own Death	5
Sharecropper	6
Self-Portrait With Seagulls	8
Barrio Secrets	9
Fourth Street Flashback	11
Dementia 101	12
Manning Up	13
Desert Flower	15
Earth Bound	16
Learning To Be A Son	18
Mexican Seascape	19
Jesus Of The Barrio	21
Self-Portrait As A Squirrel	22
Coming Home	24
Hometown Blues	26
Eve Of Destruction	27
Meeting Carmelita	28
The Sepulveda Girl	29
In Memory Of Birdie	30
In Memory Of Felix Sanchez	31
Couplets For My Truck	32
Flea Market	33
Spring And All	34
The Creek	36
The Wind In The Barrio	38
Sometimes The Evil Wind	39
New Conquistador	40
The Wall	41
if there is no tomorrow	42
Stolen Gasoline	43
The Ghost Of My Father	44
Faun	45

Houdini 46

Cordova Road 47

Tomorrow And Tomorrow
    And Tomorrow 49

Kingsbury Street Garage 51

Pinball Wizard 52

The Helicopter 53

Me At Sixteen 55

Flirting With The Past 56

Old Photograph 57

Across The Street 59

Playing With Lupita 60

The Medrano Girls 62

Matadors 64

Farmhouse 65

The Barrio Gods 66

Modern Art 67

Tortillas Brewing 68

Staying Alive 70

Come Spring 72

Hot Rod 74

Despedida 76

Abuela At The San Juan Shrine 77

The Mojado 78

White Girl 79

Sitting In My Truck 80

On The Beach 82

The Wagon 83

The Empty House 84

Blind Eye 85

Beginnings 86

Half-Horse Town 88

Envoi 90

LOVING MY ABUELO

~

Abuelo tuff as nails
the rail splitter

heaving the rusty saw
from the mill by the river

the Guadalupe River
stiff as the wind

abuelo chucking lumber
saving the square nails

I hear wood cracking
in a pile he brought home

rain soaking into a tin roof
(abuela cooking the beans to a crisp)

abuelo holding the axe
into the red sky

his biceps sweaty and salty
he picks up petrified wood in the sandhills

smiles as he tosses one
time stands still

I kiss him
as if I was a pubescent girl

BORIS KARLOFF

~

Abuela did not believe
that Boris Karloff

was really the monster
Frankenstein

could not convince her
that the bolt on his neck

came from the blacksmith
on that hill on Guadalupe St.

carefully shaped
and hammered into beauty

I tell her yes yes yes
but she says a single no

when abuela rose from her death bed
she twisted off my hands

maybe she was finally convinced
and was going to help some poor soul

ABUELO'S VISIT

~

Abuelo comes to visit me in a dream
amazed at how I have become a man

he never thought I'd accomplish anything
and of course I don't blame him

for being so pessimistic
my dreams were never about being a man

my dreams were about being a poet
I never cared for the world's trappings

I never worried about being judged
only one thing mattered

I pursued the word
as if she was a beautiful woman

I pursued the word
as if it was life itself

abuelo apologizes in the shadows
I'm bathed in light

MY OWN DEATH

~

I see my own death
in other's deaths

it's like looking in a mirror
the mirrors my abuela

would cover with a sheet
anytime someone died

a sign of respect
because it was no time

to think of the self
or so she thought

I look in the mirror
in defiance

because the self
does not belong to us

SHARECROPPER

~

Dad working the fields
as the war raged on in Europe

the corn the cotton the wheat
bitter against man

programmed to yield
even in ancient times

my dad's dark complexion
made for this kind of work

his sweaty back
rubbing against the blistering sun

the hot wind
collecting in his pockets

while over there
soldier after soldier falling dead

dad removing his hat
to let the wind in

the cool of his head
echos in my shin bones

SELF-PORTRAIT WITH SEAGULLS

~

Seagulls fly above me
like magnets

I'm all of ten stepping
just feet from the ship channel

a tugboat
spits white

the captain's face
dark as his cap

mom and dad
sit in the car

the seagull beaks
look like my dad's hook nose

all these years later
the gulf still in my shorts

BARRIO SECRETS

~

Only abuela knew my secret
the open casket

it is still us
like fallen leaves in the barrio

my guilty face
on each of those brown leaves

my school-girl sister
in the gray jeep of the sky

my brothers
log-jammed on an LA freeway

my indio father
pasted against the mountains

I push hard on the boulder
to get it off my tongue

my toothless abuela sits in the house
like a lump of coal

my hair crowns the barrio
with its shaft of light

and any moment now
time could begin

FOURTH STREET FLASHBACK

~

My aunt forces me to play Mexican bingo
in my underwear

my little nuts cold against the floor
embarrassed by La Dama

El Borrachito makes fun of me
the mermaid's top distracts me

as I put a pinto bean
on Las Jaras

when I complain that
I don't want to play anymore

my aunt beats me
with a metal coathanger

I run up and down the gravel street
oh the joys of growing up

DEMENTIA 101

~

My aunt driving off in a convertible
with her new boyfriend

in minutes he'd be digging
between her thighs on a dirt road

or under Capote Road bridge
Puente Prieto as we called it then

and we boys would jump off into the river
which seems stupid now

because it was so shallow there
and now my aunt

long married to that guy
whose dementia worsens like the world

its roundness in question
it future not assured

and the Guadalupe River still shallow
like my life

MANNING UP

~

My distant cousin three months pregnant
drops by my house

wants me to fuck her brains out
yeah my long green house

across the street from the hovel
where that old man burned to death

trying to keep warm
by making a fire in a bucket

yeah why don't you
market that you old fucker

and the other good for nothing neighbor
who stole the battery out of my car

while one of his daugthers
distracted me with her poor ass

or the short fat girl
who lay spread-eagled on my bed

I refused to fuck her nasty cunt
because she had once been

skinny and beautiful
that's really the kind of man I am

DESERT FLOWER

~

When dad took up with that
barfly from Steve's Place

well, game over y ya estufas
soon she had him by his black balls

only her daughter mattered then
she hated me most

because I was a hater
didn't pull any punches

a regular shitass I was
the fucking bitch is dead now

buried in the desert
blooming like a flower

bees won't go near
as if they were my blood relatives

EARTH BOUND

~

Mother died giving birth
father drank water

rattled in the car
the steering wheel

was a cloud in his dark hands
far away

the wind tousled my hair
my heart was a blinding white

the beast of it stumbled
across the country road

its head so flat
I cried against it

its paws so sharp
I lay against them

its eyes so bloody
I opened my mouth

mother died giving birth
and to this day

I swallow
everything she left behind

the earth
stuck in my throat like dirt

LEARNING TO BE A SON

~

The cemetery where my mother is buried
is a lonely sea

the sad eyes of fish
the forlorn swimming of whales

teardrops fill the eyes of hammerheads
a starfish won't star

the bottom of the sea
floats to the top

the storms calm themselves
the waves collapse

fish inundate the beach
I swim in the cemetery

where my mother is buried
and drown in the lonely sea

MEXICAN SEASCAPE

~

Mother bobs up and down in the sea
her name on her lapel

I sit in a black Kia Soul
the music I play is loathesome

the beach has antlers
I wave at my mother

the sea is full of trees
I can not name

mother smiles like a bowl
I put beans in

even now I am a Mexican
my eyes connected to each other by wires

I yell at mother to get out of the water
I drive like my sister

the waves cover up the sun
I am sandy and singing

mother has been dead all these years
and only the bones of the sea remain

JESUS OF THE BARRIO

~

Jesus was delusional in the barrio
he really thought he was the son of God

made promises he couldn't keep
claimed one tortilla would feed the multitudes

fought the law but the law won
was sure he would rise from the grave

insisted his mother was no whore
the barrio grew darker and darker

the sun was a heavy black ball
barrio streets ran brown with blood

the bakery offered sacred conchas
faithful old women lined up outside

but Jesus did not rise up into the sky
and settled for the barrio like the rest of us

SELF-PORTRAIT AS A SQUIRREL

~

Abuelo trapped squirrels
out in the sandhills
kept them caged at home

on the nights
when the moon went dark
abuela's plants
sour as lemons
tossed the air
between themselves

I was a teenager
lean as a palm tree
dry as dust
in a drought

my heart pumped blood
into wayward girls

it was then that I surfaced
and alarmed myself

my bushy tail
flinging piss and shit

COMING HOME

~

The junked cars and the other metals
they melted at the steel mill

whatever byproducts
they dumped into the Guadalupe

like a tree
I grew up ring by ring by ring

you can't carbon date
the future

my words thicker than blood

my hometown falling apart
like so much of my past

rusting and dripping and falling
metal becoming dirt

if I put it in my mouth
the taste of it

reduced to the single thing
we all become

HOMETOWN BLUES

~

Returning to my hometown
I feel the streets crumble in my hands

the taco hut
is made of solid rubber

my high school
has become a plump snake

I spit on an old girlfriend
to moisten her soul

when she was sixteen
she ticked like a bomb

the old barrio sports
a pile of dirty boxer shorts

my family stands
like bowling pins

EVE OF DESTRUCTION

~

Try as I might
I can not stop the destruction

I pull her panties off
she tastes like bread

my brain sits on the table
the sun is stuck in the kitchen window

the coin of her eyes so wide
I think I've swallowed her whole

she is frightened
and round as a ball

the hair on my head
cold against her belly

I hear her gasp like Christ
when the first nail was driven

MEETING CARMELITA

~

Back when I first met her
slim thighs tight lips

light-skinned redish hair
my manhood would have been

so very dark against her
like night or like the room

of doom
her thighs now

with a little more to say
her hips wider

they could easily support my weight
if I thrust against her

my manhood as hard as my life
back when I first met her

THE SEPULVEDA GIRL

~

Throwing the softball
on the gravel street

as far as the eye could see
to impress the Sepulveda girl

who lived next door
nights I sat with her

on her backdoor steps
excited and puffed up

like a bullfrog
in a stock pond

eyes as wide
and my tail as sweaty

I'd throw the softball
for all I was worth

just to see her eyes
darken with desire

IN MEMORY OF BIRDIE

~

I told Birdie let me have the tube
and as the current got ahold of him

he floated away and drowned
I went under too

but managed to get to the riverbank
the grass felt like a dark heaven

the mud between my toes
revived my guilty ass

hours later they pulled
his lifeless body out of the Guadalupe

fifty years or more have passed
I wish he wasn't dead

I hope this life I have lived
is worth something, anything

IN MEMORY OF FELIX SANCHEZ

~

Roy Orbison plays on the jukebox
I punch a guy in the face

sometimes you don't want to play pool
sometimes you just want to finish your beer

sometimes you're eyeing the girl
with that loser in cowboy boots

sometimes you don't give a damn
about Roy Orbison

the bartender tells me to get out
the punk I punched rubs his cheek

I get in my truck and head uphill
from the fairgrounds

where my buddy Felix that gentle giant
would get me through the crowds at the county fair

the Ferris wheel spinning its yarn
I wish life had a happy ending

COUPLETS FOR MY TRUCK

~

Failed human,
I dig along the bed

of my pickup truck
my gloves dirty

as if I meant
to call your name

the moon no longer tugs
at the tree in my backyard

the neighbor's horses loose
like one on my large shirts

(I should have shopped
in the boys section)

the wind spells the meadow
grateful for a chance to lay low

life is not something
we can really have like death

FLEA MARKET

~

At the flea market
two cholas wearing LA ballcaps

they block the aisle
I squeeze by

they call me
a fucking old man

I say
what does LA stand for

Lady Asses?
they give me a deadly look

call me an asshole
oh I say

so the LA stands for
Lady Assholes

you never know what you'll find
at the flea market

SPRING AND ALL

~

When Zhivago crumbles
of heart attack behind the tram

I am no help
and imagine friends

who have passed on
never to taste of Lara again

my friend Jim
never to see his daughter grow up

my step son
dying young

leaving behind
blossoming daughters

life become cold like snow
when we go

cobblestone street
welcomes the good doctor

as if there was no summer
after spring

THE CREEK

~

I play in the flooded creek
by my house

cut a gash on my heel
mother pours alcohol on it

wraps it with a rag
I still have the scar to prove it

I don't have
my mother anymore to prove it

the old house is gone
the creek has changed little

I poke out my head
between the cracks of time

and feel its two broken edges
squeeze me as if I was being born

the creek is dry now
and the rocks sit waiting like always

nothing is more out of our hands
than the past

THE WIND IN THE BARRIO

~

The wind in the barrio
blows away your sighs

the wind in the barrio
makes you close your eyes

the wind in the barrio
warns you of the danger

when the cops are prowling
the wind will let you know

when the gang is rolling
the wind will bring their stench

the wind in the barrio
caresses your sweet thighs

the wind in the barrio
blows away the lies

the wind in the barrio
is all I've ever wanted

SOMETIMES THE EVIL WIND

~

Sometimes an evil wind
blows through the barrio

buries its head
in the dead

sometimes it skips over you
like a blinded storm cloud

sometimes the bakery windows
shatter and release sweetness

sometimes it knocks down clocks
sometimes it pulls down your socks

sometimes it spares the rod
sometimes it buries itself in sod

sometimes the barrio sighs
or loses an eye

sometimes when there's no wind
even the innocent will sin

NEW CONQUISTADOR

~

I repeat the crimes
of my ancestors

half-boiled caldos
indecent chile

the beans still hard
uncooked tortillas

the sad-eyed fiesta
the silent grito

the revolution which
accomplishes nothing

I am only the flesh
and blood that always was

and for that
I must not be proud

yet may my words
fight on

THE WALL

~

There's no wall around the barrio
only a broom sweeping you back in

a cloud of dust
settles on your conchas

a cloud of dust
settles on your barbacoa tacos

a cloud of dust
settles on your gangbangers

a cloud of dust settles on the dog
chained in the backyard

there's no wall around the barrio
only the broom that lowers the boom

a cloud of dust settles on the cholas
whose jeans are way too tight

a cloud of dust settles on the barrio
and its tears turn the dust to mud

a gust of wind will dry it out
that's what the barrio's all about

~~if there is tomorrow~~
~~it is only borrowed~~
~~and as for yesterday~~
~~every dog has his day~~

sometimes your past
and your future
meet up with each other
and destroy themselves

STOLEN GASOLINE

~

When dad was low on gas money
he'd take me with him

on the dark dirt field roads
half a mile to the man's farmhouse

the one he sharecropped for
and in the middle of the night

he'd fill two gas cans
from the farmer's storage tanks

and this is way back when
gas was twenty-six cents a gallon

that shows you how poor we were
the night was as black as oil

with the smell of stolen gasoline
the theft reminds me fondly of my father

THE GHOST OF MY FATHER

~

The ghost of my father
white as a sheet

bony like the moon
briny like Salton Sea

scares me
and then laughs

sharp teeth retreat
into a smile

he flaps his wings
smiles a deadly smile

and then laughs again
just kidding, son, he says

I hug and kiss him
because a father is forever

FAUN

~

Dad lying in the hospital
with a tumor in his head

the operation is a slim
to none affair

dad dreams of the mountains
and desert of Indio

Salton Sea a dirty mirror
grapes clinging desperately to vines

the purple Mexican laborers
the sun dimpled like a golf ball

the surgeon comes out
to say dad didn't make it

high up in the San Gabriel Mountains
I see dad fight off the snow storm

and a faun urging him,
"Come on, this way, this way."

HOUDINI

~

Memories of my mother
are hard to come by

since she died
when I was twelve

a day
after Christmas Day

cold evening
at my Uncle Juan's house

I cried not knowing
what death really meant

over the weeks and months
it begin to sink in

not even Houdini
comes back

CORDOVA ROAD

~

The earliest memory of a girl:
we were tumbling around

in a trailer half-full of cotton
on Cordova Road

her marvelous scent
still stuck in my head

don't remember her name
her dark features

or the feel of her thighs
as we wrestled and giggled

my mother on the other side
of the cotton field

pulling a heavy cotton sack
the sun so round and heavy

it almost fell out of the sky
our little lives cling to that very sun

screaming as we plummet
past the past

TOMORROW AND TOMORROW
AND TOMORROW
~

Late 1950's
though he sharecropped

and did mechanic work
dad would get that wild hair up his ass

when cotton time rolled around---
living in small shacks

most filled with Braceros
we wandered the state

north and south
La Mesa up north for cotton

Comanche up north for pecans
El Maton along the coast for cotton

ah the life of a seasonal worker
and then he'd bring us back

back to Seguin to sharecrop
or work for David Perez

at David's garage by Reanau Brother's
bloody chicken plant

today the plant
is owned by Tyson

tomorrow and tomorrow and tomorrow
do not matter to *ayer*

KINGSBURY STREET GARAGE

~

My father dismantled
and stacked engine parts

his hands greasy
and knowing the sum of all evil

as anyone who works
at a junkyard knows

removing a carburetor for him
the wrench slipped

and I cut my finger
blood mixing with oil

father just shrugged his shoulders
and continued lifting the V-8 out of a Ford

silhouetted against the sky
I felt it would soar like a bird

but it came back down to the ground
without a sound

PINBALL WIZARD

~

Saturday nights I'd walk
five blocks to the White House Drive In

a hamburger joint with carhops
the hot spot on the west side of town

the cars circled around
went back to town and came back again

round and round they'd go
cursed the small town boredom

some nights I'd meet
Larry Nieto there

he played the pinball machine
like a pinball wizard

but no kind of wizard
would ever stay in this town for long

THE HELICOPTER

~

I was flying my make-believe helicopter
on top of the chicken coop

I was maybe eight
the fields stretched

for as far as the eyes could see
the rise and fall of the creek

the creek I played in wet or dry
the Huber kid

up to his waist in quicksand
the chickens annoyed

that I was making
helicopter noises overhead

would only quiet down
when mom fed them

I lay the controls down
on the tin roof

climbed down and ate
my share of pilot beans

they bounced inside my belly
like bullets in a foreign war

ME AT SIXTEEN

~

At sixteen I catch myself
running a fine-tooth comb thru my life

mom dead four years now
dad having abandoned me

he's run off with some woman
he met at a bar

the comb glides thru my hair
molecules spark and shine

a single hair
can become vast universes

my life falls like dandruff
on the sheet of paper

that I will eventually
write it on

FLIRTING WITH THE PAST

~

I flirt with my past
as if it was a pretty girl

red lips beautiful eyes
brown eyes and hair

hips to match her lips
thighs to match her eyes

I flirt with my past
to make it last

I flirt with my past
because it was a blast

I don't know what the future will hold
copper or gold

I keep the past in my head
like every book I've ever read

OLD PHOTOGRAPH

~

In torn Army pants
and Army t-shirt

I stand next
to an old washing machine

in the backyard
of my abuela's house

my bicycle leans
against the tree

I used to climb
as a kid

the shed you see
behind me

is where I used to fondle
my neighbor Juanita's breasts

when we were teens
she was a little chubby

but her smile
made up for that

[58]

ACROSS THE STREET

~

Across the street
Meme is washing his Mustang

it's yellow with a black vinyl top
while in abuela's front yard

the chinaberry tree
is dropping all its balls

I used to sit up
in that tree on Halloween

and throw water balloons
on unsuspecting trick o treaters

the tree is long gone now
and so is abuela

the barrio has buried
its head in yesterday

somehow I have managed to stay
just ahead of the past

PLAYING WITH LUPITA

~

Who would have thought
that of Lupita

as we ran up to the Zorn House
which was falling apart in those days

Juan Seguin Elementary
just across the creek

where we Mexicans
had to attend school

white schools being
off limits to us

the Zorn House was
a forbidden place too

since it was crumbling
just like our dark brown lives

chasing Lupita's skinny little thighs
back then

who would have thought
Lupita would become a man

THE MEDRANO GIRLS

~

It's summer and the Medrano girls
are in their backyard

I walk to Blumberg Park
which is a block from abuela's house

the swing is broken
the seesaw boards lie on the ground

caddy corner to the park
sits Munche's Grocery Store

(the barrio convenience store)
where you can buy a single cigarette

my aunt sent me to buy them all the time
on Newton Street nearby

they sold drugs then and now
no apples fall on Newton yards

not that anybody on that street
could offer much gravity

Don Abel is home from work now
and the Medrano girls are back inside

I had a crush on one of them
I forget which one

MATADORS

~

You used to call me
Black Boy

because I was
such a dark Mexican

you went on
to become a politician

remember when you
and your buddies

would rush the field
after a Matador game

to feel up
the cheerleaders

I stayed in the stands
and marveled at the score

FARMHOUSE

~

Playing alone out in the fields
beyond our farmhouse

or in the dirt creek
whose walls I dug out

to make caves
which sometimes

crumbled down on me
I trapped ground squirrels

I'd take the rodents home
they made good captives

I feel sorry for them
sixty years later is no attonement

our farmhouse leveled now
like all the past

pounded into the ground
to make room for the future

THE BARRIO GODS

~

The barrio doesn't owe me a thing
so we are even

the gravel streets I swallowed whole
the schools I plundered

the friends I lost to barrio wars
the sweetness which grew wild

I drank my fill of life
there was no cure at all

the girls I made love to
spilled at the fiesta

the cops combed the barrio
for lice and vice

if the barrio gods are looking down on me
tell them to set me free

MODERN ART

~

Leaving Mike's house
Pete pops a wheelie on his Honda

he breaks his arm in the fall
the moon looks like a bone in the sky

his arm in a cast
the Army takes him anyway

to fight that flimsy war in Viet Nam
for some reason the orange color

of his motorcycle gas tank
lingers in my head

the asphalt his elbow twisted
his helmet scratched and brimming

and then so very far away
the Vietnamese girl he courted with cigarettes

at the ammunition dump
he was blown apart like modern art

TORTILLAS BREWING

~

Tortillas brewing on the stove
abuela's dark Indian nose silhouetted

against my life
my life bubbling over like boiling beans

the first girl I ever loved
Carmen Gonzales

cousin to my best friend Pete
as a little girl she walked

the gravel street to her cousin's house
wearing only panties (no breasts yet)

things were different back in the Fifties
my uncircumcised libido

still knew what was up
even though I myself didn't have a clue

nothing like a hot tortilla
and those dark black spots

the butter slides over
my heart skips a beat remembering that

STAYING ALIVE

~

Seguin is buried
just like its namesake

deep in my heart
Seguin has betrayed me

and I have betrayed it
as a twelve year old

it held promise
but even then it struggled

in my head
I painted it bright

with golden streets
and shady parks

the dusty barrio reared
its ugly head at times

yet even then
I stayed afloat

and grabbed it
by the throat

COME SPRING

~

I was born in a cold farmhouse
in the middle of winter

surrounded by fields
which lay fallow

patiently waiting
for the planting season

when the corn would sprout
and the sorghum break thru ground

the cotton will soon be
white in a corner of the field

my father sharecropped
and mother lorded over

in her sunbonnet
which she made herself

and I who fail
to pass on the seed

come spring
the fields will question me

HOT ROD

~

Third grade at
Jefferson Avenue Elementary

dad would show up
at noon

in a one of a kind
hot rod

built by him
and David Perez

he'd show up
at noon

just to bring
my lunch

how could I
not be special

and yet I wish
I could tell dad

dad those are
great memories

God help me
my past is almost full

DESPEDIDA

~

A camarada and me after we've had
one too many virongas

Ese, mi abuela made the best
fried beans,

don't be telling me that your pinche abuela
made better fried beans

because I will bust
your fucking ass!

They came out crispy as hell,
made with a shitload of manteca.

No, bitch, your abuela's beans
were second rate, cabron.

I'm not gonna tell you again, ese,
te voy a dar en la madre so shut up!

N'ombre, culero,mi abuela made the best
goddamn fucking fried beans ever, bitch!

ABUELA AT THE SAN JUAN SHRINE

~

On her knees in San Juan
trying to prove to God

trying to prove to the Lord
trying to prove to La Virgen

that she can be thankful
and do penance

do justice where justice
is due and deemed

at her age she was tuff
as the nails which pinned Jesus

I can not fathom
how deep her faith ran

that it rises in me
yet falls to the ground

she knew well all my sins
and intercedes even now

THE MOJADO

~

Dad tells mom
"Nom'bre, el mojadito
got himself killed by the tractor
after I told him

over and over again
ten quidado" be very careful

I told the boss
and the boss said goddamnit to hell

another one bites the dust
trying to make a living out of dirt

in this godforsaken country
which is what my dad

called Texas and its surroundings
as if it was true

mother se persino
and I wondered which mojado

WHITE GIRL

~

My first white girl
blonde

the night dragging itself
into dawn

the moon shedding its skin
towards the sun

new cars at the Chevrolet dealer
bright like stars

our juices intermingled
as we slept

in the morning I go home
in thick fog

the past is a whirlpool
sucking me into

the quicksand
of the hourglass

SITTING IN MY TRUCK

~

I'm riding my bicycle back from
the mail box

it's a warm winter day
on the farm on Huber Road

in the distance I see
my Aunt Duvina backing up

the car from our driveway
she's taking mama to have her baby

both mama and baby boy
died that day in a country doctor's office

as I write this sitting in my truck
the scent of wild flowers is strong

and I wonder if it's mama
sending me a message

the sun digs into my hand
through the open truck window

I feel at peace as if
I was back in my mother's womb

ON THE BEACH

~

My footprints on Padre
the waves pile up like pillows

an outbound freighter
seems painted against the sky

a jellyfish huffs and puffs
among other jelly fish

on the beach a man-of-war
has met its match

I must be eight years old
seagulls take the bread

if I tossed my life into the air
they would take it, too

instead here I am
an old man in an old shadow

I gather the sand in my hand
it spills through my fingers like time

THE WAGON

~

A wagon fell on my abuelo Fidencio
and killed him

out there on Cordova Road
where horned toads hid in the ditch

where my mother told us kids
a headless lady rode a carriage

nearby Don Jose
worked the cane fields

with his dick
hard for my mother

but he was too much of gentleman
Mexico had spoiled him he said

abuelo Fidencio buried there
along Highway 46

like so much of my family
a fucking family reunion

THE EMPTY HOUSE

~

Growing up there was never
civilized furniture

in our house
though all our neighbors

had moved into
the 20th century

abuela insisted
on raising us the old-fashioned way

this after our father had dumped
my brothers and my sister on her lap

abuelo drank every weekend
and abuela waited hopelessly

the pinche viejita
thought that was alright

she never saw the light
I never thought it was alright until now

BLIND EYE

~

I passed along my seed
as La Virgen decreed

can not guarantee the outcome
not every sunrise offers sun

my family lived off the land
I had no such plan

I lived from day to day
my feet were made of clay

I turned a blind eye on the future
and you see what it got me

BEGINNINGS

~

A once white snowball
comes rolling down

from the San Gabriel Mountains
towards my father's house

gathering desert sand
it becomes brown and dirty

father brushes it aside
with his dark hand

his wife and his son
dead a decade ago

the doom suspended
in cold desert air

the mountains cast
giant self-conscious shadows

my father looks good
in a long-sleeve black shirt

at night his balls rage
against his new, young wife

[87]

HALF-HORSE TOWN

~

My half-horse town
lacked the whole enchilada

streets shed their dust on me
I froze in the elada

it chased my dreams away
with nightmares

my half-horse town
had neither heads nor tails

abuela defended it
the best she could

but abuela also claimed that Jesus
was allergic to nails

she hurried to church
in a dressed-down lurch

I can't be dragged down
by this sad clown town I tell her

I tell abuela
que la vida me la pela

ENVOI

~

That stump you see rotting
come rain or shine

once proudly held
its arms out

to welcome day
and night

lent its youthful branches
to bird or bug

offered a bouquet
of leaves to the wind

displayed sweet shade
to man and beast alike

to take a break
whether from joy or sorrow

now sadly waits
for no tomorrow

suffers the fate
we all must face

when time has had enough
of us

Reyes Cárdenas was born and raised in Seguin, Texas. He is the author of *Anti-Bicicleta Haiku* (1976), *Survivors of the Chicano Titanic* (1981), *Elegies For John Lennon* (1984, 2006), *I Was Never A Militant Chicano* (1986), *Chicano Poet: 1970–2010* (2013), and Tortured Barrio Songs (2019).